AN EYE-OPENING

ADVENTURE

GATOR!

LAWRENCE T. MAHONEY
Photographs by
RICHARD BENSON

TEN SPEED PRESS

BERKELEY, CALIFORNIA

TEN SPEED PRESS
P. O. Box 7123 • Berkeley, California 94707

Photographs © 1991 by Richard Benson
Cover and text design by Ken Scott
Composition by Ann Flanagan Typography

Library of Congress Cataloging-in-Publication Data
Mahoney, Lawrence.
Gator! / Lawrence T. Mahoney.
p.   cm.
ISBN 0-89815-404-9
1. Alligators—Florida. 2. Alligators—Florida—Anecdotes.
3. Florida—Social life and customs—Anecdotes.   I. Title.
QL666.C925M34   1991   90-49738
597.98—dc20   CIP

First printing, 1991

Printed in South Korea
1 2 3 4 5 — 95 94 93 92 91

DEDICATION

To Jim Morrison of The Doors, ·
Florida boy who became
the Lizard King.

50,000 German tourists came to Florida in 1989
to enjoy the weather and see two things:
the rockets at the Cape and the gators.

Two gators lounge in duckweed under the noonday sun. Largely nocturnal,
gators do most of their moving around at night.

P R O L O G U E

Although this is an account about great creatures of the mud, who, even more than the sun, are the symbol of Florida,

I first look skyward because part of Florida has become a wasteland, a cross between L.A. and the New Jersey Turnpike. Despite all the green of money and trees, Florida has become an Egypt instead of a Promised Land, and it was people caused it, not gators or the sun.

Why, fifty thousand German tourists came here in 1989 alone, to enjoy the weather and see two major things: the rockets at the Cape and the gators at various tourist attractions and loose in the Glades. These critters are so strange and beautiful. Being a semi-Cracker, I could cry about it, but a swig of Haitian rum will do for that. A swig and a look away from interstates, Burger Kings, motels, Disney World, schoolhouses that look like road prisons, and the new housing of concrete and fiberboard—all so contemptible and so far removed from God, from the natural life and mud habitat of our symbol, the gator.

This region of Florida was among the last mapped
in the United States.

This book is a long journey and it begins, I suppose, where I'm watching the sky on the banks of Lake Okeechobee, Florida's inland sea and the source of the Everglades. Twenty-two miles beyond Clewiston, headquarters of U.S. Sugar and at once America's sweetest and nastiest town, you come to the Fisheating Creek Bridge, where the wild waterway makes its final rush to the great lake. I have been told by an old feller in a trailer park that an inordinate number of eight-foot gators live around this natural aquatic intersection, these being the most mobile and potentially mean of the species.

This region of inner Florida was among the last mapped out in the United States. This happened during the Seminole Wars, during which elements of the U.S. Navy, often a seaman poling a flat-bottom boat accompanied by the infantry, sought out the ever-fighting, ever-retreating half-breed Indians from a place renamed Georgia, where there are gators, but not like down here. Imagine the swamp sailor or the army lieutenant who discovered the Indian name for this place, where fish were eaten by alligators and men and snakes and ospreys: *ThlothlopokaHatchee*.

Today, with 76 percent of this land sacked, or about to be, along with the symbol of it all, well, I just sigh and look up. Across the dying lake with its blue-algae version of the plague from dairy cow runoff, to put it politely, and over there toward the misnamed Gold Coast, a range of cumulus clouds becomes a massive cumulonimbus, promising rain and hail, thunder and lightning. When it can rise no farther, the cloud forms into a giant anvil the size of Fort Lauderdale, a noncity born during the Seminole hostilities that will soon be bigger than Miami. Below, large clouds hang together like a giant udder from the base of the sky mountains. Obscured in gray, the udders open.

No ponies here!
At a Gainesville mall, a girl hangs onto a friendly gator.

A lottery to save the gator?

I walk fitfully on the shore littered with aluminum cans, plastic bottles, spent rifle shells, and broken lighters. One of the eight-foot gators of Fisheating Creek materializes in the rain, his jaws agape. I take it that he is drinking from the sky I'm watching. I turn my head up and me and the gator share a drink. Only I follow mine with a gulp of rum and then salute the gator with the bottle when he figures out a human is too close and moves away.

As a Floridian, I find the alligator a beautiful swimmer and cannot adjust to the fact that there are now too many of them here. My image of gators collided with reality in the fall of 1988, during Florida's gator hunt. This book is an eyewitness account of how gators are both an obsession and a source of fear for Floridians in general, from the Tamiami Trail to Lake Talquin.

Expeditions are often frightening. They can also be affirming. Follow me as I follow the gator in Florida, through a time when our beautiful swimmer was subjected to a lottery, a lottery to save the gator.

The author inspects a dead gator in the slaughter house.

Lawrence Mahoney
Miami, May 1989

*You'll always find good people and tall tales at the GatorKicks bar
on the edge of the Everglades.*

CONTENTS

Lieutenant Huffstodt of the Game and Fresh Water Fish Commission briefs reporters and photographers before the hunt.

THE HUNT
AND THE SLAUGHTERHOUSE

Since September 2, 1961, Florida has had a statewide closed season protecting all alligators. Widespread hunting had taken a tremendous toll on the population, and the alligator was facing near-extinction in some southeastern states before protective legislation was passed in the 1950s and 1960s. As a result of this closed season, the alligator population did, in fact, increase, but to such an extent that Florida then faced the problem of alligator *over*population. The state's response to this was to reopen the season, for a short time allowing the harvesting of its gators.

This is the story of how for one month, September 1988, Florida sanctioned night hunts of the gator, dusk to dawn, with no firearms allowed save short bangsticks, which are usually used to kill sharks. The hunt, or harvest, or lottery, captured the attention of the world.

There was a bloodlust not only from anticipating the killing of the unsuspecting official prey, but also from speculation that a hunter or two, or maybe a boatload of journalists, would be swallowed up in those gaping pink and white jaws. Wah-hoo, boys, let's sharpen up those homemade harpoons and get out the axes, clubs, knives, nooses, spears, spear guns, grappling hooks, and all the duct tape you can rustle up.

Photographer Richard Benson and I are free-lancers representing a very small Washington news agency. We are getting desperate because the sun is going down on Alligator Alley, the dangerous two-lane, cross-peninsula highway. The state Game and Fresh Water Fish boys are

Duct tape protects hunters from powerful jaws.

having a kickoff on the highway named for the quarry, and we can't find any sign of it. To the north of the Alley a great new interstate highway pushes east, steel cranes flying, turning the immediate Everglades into ugly mini–mountain ranges of marl and coral rock.

Gail Campbell of the Washington Times stands out with her souvenir hat reading:

"I Ain't Afraid of No Lizard Now!"

I recall a German short story's way of saying it: "It was a long, long road long." We are now looking for a hot dog stand and the state of Florida's Gator Lottery kickoff. We find them at the same canal-side spot, looking south to a sea of saw grass.

Here will take place the formal initiation of the rites of the hunt, the first gator hunt sanctioned by Florida in twenty years. The construction base camp is forested with television live eyes. Journalists from fifty countries are here for the spectacle. Turkey vultures circle on thermals above the hot pavement. A lone gator, looking not unlike Albert of the *Pogo* comic strip, peers from the canal, the water losing its fight with hydralia. We buy Jolt colas from the Greek hot dog man and settle in for the opening, which is timed for, naturally, the six o'clock news. A big American flag flies overhead, near a wheelless blue Chevy overturned in the sand.

A bulky old fellow in shorts and a VFW hat comes over to me and squats in the grass. "Last time they did something like this, the hunters almost started killing each other," he says, then stands up to follow a pretty newscaster. A hunter tells us that the news saturation is resented and implies that there might be some accidents if the journalists follow the hunt into the swamps and canals, sort of like the cuffing of the American journalists in Grenada by the American command, letting them know who is boss.

Video crews tape other video crews going into the Everglades.

Gail Campbell of the *Washington Times* stands out with her souvenir hat from another kind of lizard hunt. On its peak are the words "I Ain't Afraid of No Lizard Now! Scrape Ore, S.C." Wait till Gail sees our lizards. Another Washington reporter, Myra MacPherson, is known for her book on the Vietnam War and which class of Americans got killed and maimed in it. A lot of the men on the Alley this opening night are wearing remnants of Vietnam, jungle boots and the like. I've got on baggy fatigue pants and a Courvoisier black baseball cap with a red hog pin in it for the Arkansas troops I worked with during the Mariel sealift. I'm also wearing the largest buck knife ever seen in Vietnam, made for a PFC by his grandpappy from a file; it makes Crocodile Dundee's seem diminutive. With my legal pad, the outfit confuses a camera crew from Fuji News Network in Japan, three camera operators led by beautiful Eiko Mitcke from Tokyo. She thinks I'm in charge, much to the amusement of the wildlife officials. She also can't understand why alligators are being hunted in America, there being only two in Japan, children's heroes in zoos. I hope that her video showing my knife doesn't make it back to Japan. Eiko and her crew will see some real gator killers tonight.

Everyone gathers at Everglades Holiday Park, a tourist attraction in far-western Broward County. Lieutenant Jim Huffstodt, a Midwesterner who is the only wildlife officer not wearing a .38, tells us there will be unmarked units prowling the Glades this first day of the thirty-day hunt. A Cessna makes a low swoop, the word "wildlife" painted under its wings. As dark comes, the lights of Fort Lauderdale and Miami can be seen on the southeast horizon. A few small gators play around the floating pier, waiting for more handouts of Kentucky Fried Chicken from a family with young children. Lieutenant Huffstodt admits that "photo opportunities" are few. The press, of course, grows impatient. Folks who live at Holiday Park are worried that someone is going to harpoon Ol' One Eye, a big tourist attraction. There is rifle fire from the nearby Everglades, unexplained shooting.

Ron Lopez, a journalist from the *London Sun*, produces a bottle of fine Haitian Barbancourt Rhum and gives it to me. With that and my knife I am more relaxed than the broadcast journalists, who are itchy about approaching deadlines and the first gator not yet taken. The stars are brilliant, the saw grass lovely, and the frog charms almost orchestral. I talk to a German photographer, Ursula Seemann, who wears an All Access sticker on her right breast. She has just come from taking photographs of Hai-

tian boat people being interdicted by George Bush's coast guard. Looking for gators, Ursula, from two-thousand-year-old Trion on the Mosel, is fatigued.

More of the Barbancourt and I follow a young gator gracefully swimming off the dock. Carpenter Tony Lewark of Fort Lauderdale, wearing fatigue pants and a black motorcycle shirt, puts his Mon Ark Three boat on the ramp. Spear gun in hand, he is crowded by the impatient press. "No," he says, "I've never hunted gator before. No, I won't tell you how much the boat and rig costs—my wife might find out. I'm out here all the time, but I've never trapped a gator." Lewark disappears in the saw grass–lined darkness of the canal.

The newscaster from Channel 4's unmarked car, who looks like Charlotte Rampling, alerts us: Trappers have just taken the first one, and midnight is approaching. They're over at Sawgrass, a nearby recreational area. We scramble, me sick on drink, Ursula, and the September stars.

The trappers are from Pembroke Pines. Dawn Mackey, twenty-four, in pink shorts, snagged the eight-and-a-half-

A Hendry County officer checks on the catch as hunters return from Lake Okeechobee.

A tired Ross Hooks looks over his catch at 1:30 A.M. after a long night on the lake.

Ross Hooks and part of his extensive gator collection.

Ross and Weezie Hooks skin one of many gators processed in their slaughterhouse during the hunt.

footer. Her husband, Doug Mackey, twenty-four, and friend, Steve Prater, twenty-seven, helped in the fight to pull it in. The men are saying they're going to call each other Crocodile Mackey and Alligator Prater. Children dance around the duct-taped gator, saying, "You'll be alright, Mr. Gator!" Dawn, holding a rubber gator head, has a four-month-old son named Danny and is a housekeeper. "Poor Mr. Gator, I feel so sorry for you," an unidentified child crows in the night.

Lieutenant Huffstodt runs up, breathless, and says, "These are the first!" Another has arrived by this time at Sawgrass. The gators are piled into a metallic red pickup truck for the trip to Ross and Weezie Hooks's processing plant on Peaceful Ridge Road in Davie. Huffstodt's radio reports another one taken ashore at Holiday Park. I go to the plant, where I find myself in the slaughterhouse with Dawn, and a black gator tied up like a prisoner with its limbs behind its back and its eyes covered with duct tape, along with a dozen previously captured gators.

The slaughterhouse is a concrete storage building built in the fifties. There is an Air Force steel survival .22 for the execution of the musky, fearful gators, black and piled in a little compound on top of one another, harpooned, hosed down, mouths taped. The place reeks of fear and pain, like a police station. Tony Lewark brings in a twelve-footer, to the delight of the accompanying camera crew. Dawn doesn't look too well and I need some Barbancourt. A nine-foot-gator tries to scale the concrete block pen.

The actual cutting up is done in a tiny adjacent building with a state alligator control boat on the side. It is like a mortician's room. There is a bucket of blood. I feel the softness of a gator hide. They are cut behind the ears for bleeding.

Weezie Hooks, Ross's wife and partner, comes in. She is Ross's second wife. They know each other from high school. The first wife didn't care a thing about gators, but Weezie wields a knife in the slaughterhouse. Weezie says, "We've got eight—make that nine—coming in. Ross is whipped, twenty hours of sleep in the last week."

In their home, I note the decor: the huge central room contains a stuffed gator hand, various skulls, two stuffed red foxes, a homecoming '86 Tennessee plaque, and an Indian corn braid. There is a full cayman skin on the wall of their daughter's room. I think at first that it's a gator, but brilliant little Jennifer points out the identifying cayman bumps on the hatching baby alligators on her cute T-shirt. The Hooks show me charms made of teeth and claws, skulls, stuffed heads, bags of loose teeth and claws. Ross says, "We never throw away a head. If not used we let it rot until the teeth fall out. Some toenails are white, some are brown, some gunmetal."

Weezie talks of a phone call from two boys, who are holding gators in their mom's kitchen. With the money they make from the hunt, they're gonna buy her a house with a swimming pool—"to keep gators in, of course." Weezie shows us Ross's belt, made by Navajo Leo, who comes and takes gator remains and returns with belts, one at a time. Ross's buckle is made with turquoise and two huge stained gator teeth. They're from a gator that almost killed him. He tells the story:

"There is *no such thing* as an unloaded gun or a dead gator. We leave their jaws taped on the dissecting table. This was a road kill about 10:30 at night. The gator turned out to not be quite dead when we pulled it up on the table. About halfway up, it started going for me, thrashing out

Hooks's assistants Cheryl Russell and Barry Holdridge roll an alligator skin in salt before shipping it to a hide auction.

from the dead. Damned thing spinned and rolled and gouged out my arm even though the mouth was taped. The proverbial unloaded gun; the proverbial dead alligator. And this happened with experienced trappers. Even after death, muscles move—and strongly." Ross had had to be on antibiotics for infection from the bites.

Ross tells me an urban gator tale about his daughter, Jennifer. She was riding in the truck with him, when she ran into fearful folk. There was this little three-footer, and a big cop had a gun drawn, which was itself longer than the poor little gator. Jennifer pleaded, "Daddy, Daddy, can I take it, can we take it inside the truck with us?" Ross agreed and taped the mouth. Jennifer slung the gator over her shoulder. The cop reholstered his special.

"There is no such thing as an unloaded gun or a dead gator."

Ross then shows me a big stuffed head of a fourteen-and-a-half-footer that went after a little boy at Everglades Holiday Park. "A campground, you know, where people live all the time." The boy had a bag of stinking chicken livers and was on the floating dock. The gator slid up on the dock, blocking the boy from the exit. The kid hit the water. The gator jumped in right behind him. The boy swam to shore, screaming; the big gator followed, snapping. It was then that the residents decided to have the gator removed. Ross took him alive on a baited hook.

Ross brings out two small stuffed heads to make a point. "This'll show you the difference between farm gators and wild ones. See, this wild one is lean and mean and ready to go to work. The farm feller has much thinner leather skin, doesn't have the opportunity to grow and meet regular feeding flesh. It grows wide. Also, the farm gator loses teeth from eating on one side of the mouth all the time and striking concrete."

Ross grew up in central Florida in Clermont, where his family is in the history books for settling the town. Polio was responsible for his limp; his good knee was bitten by another "dead" gator. He is forty-four and country handsome. "Alligators were not that common when I was growing up. They had been worked on pretty hard. My dad was an avid hunter, and could call animals. I had baby gators as pets, hatched twelve or thirteen by myself, and fooled with them in a big marsh in front of my house." His hands are stubby, scarred. "I have trapped nuisance gators for over ten years. The population growth in Florida has been incredible. You know, I see these bodies of water in housing developments and by shopping centers and I know there are gators in them, but you never see them. They are completely nocturnal, and the people twenty feet away are not even aware that the gator is there. Once, as a boy, I was fishing. I fell asleep in the boat with my feet hanging over. An uncle drove by on the highway and started yelling at me. An eight- or nine-foot gator was just watching my feet and cruising closer to them. That ol' gator was just watching."

We are in the slaughterhouse on a Saturday afternoon. The smell of a dead ten-footer pervades the Australian pines and horse stables. Assistant Cheryl Russell, in socks and black shoes and skintight shorts, pushes up the sliding garage door and enters the little building where Weezie and Ross are cutting up two gators. There is duct tape over the eyes of the gator. Feel how soft his skin is.

The wife to the fatigued husband: "You gonna skin all night again tonight?" The heavy man with the pipe and beard has blank eyes: "Oh I would rather spend twelve hours hunting 'em out on the lake than in this shed."

Cheryl Russell, mother of two, with Weezie since age fourteen, talks of being an archer and going deer hunting with her husband. I hand her my big gator skull and take the cigarette from her mouth. "Oh crush it," she says. The photographer walks her to the shade. Click. We talk of making her Diana of the gator hunt.

Jesse Kennon shows his custom-made gator ring.

A tourist, a game warden, and a gator's all got about the same size brain. Just a little bigger than a good-size peanut.

— HARRY CREWS, *Florida Frenzy*

CHAPTER 2

FOR PEOPLE WHO LIKE TO EAT GATOR TAIL

It distinctly does not taste like chicken. Alligator meat, of which there is a glut from Florida's 1988 hunting season, tastes instead like veal

or the kind of white barbeque you get at the genuine smoky rib places in North Carolina or Georgia. But Coopertown, Florida, is not of the South. Miami is only fifteen minutes away, and most of the folks who partake of Sally and Jesse Kennon's Everglades cuisine at the Coopertown Restaurant are from places like Toronto or Frankfurt. Sally's Gator Bits should go national, just as Bojangles did. Or international, competing with Burger King in London or McDonald's on the Kufuerstendamn. The restaurant itself has undergone a recent remodeling, mostly from the muscles of Jesse Kennon, a pure Celt from the boot-heel extension of Missouri. His gator jewelry will knock your eyes

out. He and Sally and the other six residents of Coopertown underline in a culinary way what America is all about. Don't leave it all to the Germans and Canadians—

Gator tail and frogs' legs at Coopertown Restaurant.

go eat some gator or frog legs yourself at the Coopertown Restaurant and be fortified with the good earth of the southernmost state.

Sally, as head cook and waitress, is coy about her recipe, just like the late Kentucky Colonel. I found out, however, that she does use Martha White Corn Meal, a staple in kitchens from Lima, Ohio, to Dublin, Georgia.

While Jesse and a group of men examine a shiny twenty-two-passenger, made-in-Miami airboat to add to his fleet, Sally offers me a Dr. Pepper and talks about cookin' good for busloads of tourists from Bremen. Once she was a soldier's wife in Worms, Germany, so she is handy with German in addition to Spanish, from the Miami Cubans, and French, from the Quebec Gaullists.

Underneath the stuffed head of a fourteen-and-a-half-foot gator, with marble eyes made in Europe, Sally says that she deep-fries the chunks of meat with a lot of spices and serves them up for $6.95 with garlic bread or coleslaw. Should you want more gator, you can order the Everglades Sampler, which is a combination dinner of six frog legs, one-third pound of gator tail, coleslaw, french fries, and garlic bread. Wash it down with a Heineken or Löwenbräu for $1.75 (cheapest in all greater Miami), and your total tab for being a minor glutton in the storied Everglades will come to under $20.

Having eaten, swig down another Löwenbräu or a Pepsi Cola and get Jesse or one of his men to take you on an airboat ride into the Glades. In some ways, it beats taking a Land Rover through the brush in the African shadow of Kilimanjaro. The tariff is easy, $8.50 per head.

If you don't want to go out in the half-airplane/half-boat to see living gators, kites, otters, water snakes (poisonous and not), the world's most stunning assortment of birdlife, and perhaps a Florida panther, deer, or black bear, ask Sally if she has time, while the table is being cleared, to tell you about the frogs' legs.

"Well, they are hunted at night," she says. "They, not gator tail, are the specialty of the house. The hunter sits high in his seat in his one-man Everglades airboat. He's got a lot of equipment. A headlamp like a miner. A gig and a sack for the frogs. Sometimes he's out there until 2:00 or 3:00 in the morning. You can hear him coming to the dock from miles away. He hands the bag to me, and I prepare them for the customer. You know, I am famous all over the world—in France, Germany, Austria, and New York—for my frogs' legs. They come out here and make TV and movies about us." Mm-mm-good with Louisiana Tabasco sauce.

I'm full of gator and frogs' legs and have just bought a postcard of a Florida snakebird to send home. "The Everglades, You'll Visit Again." A Hell's Angel from Florida City wheels his black Harley ever so carefully by a wounded five-foot alligator lying on the tarmac of Ned's Bait and Tackle next door, where extremely nervous hunters are getting gas. His name is Jens, and he wears an aviator death's head on his chest and a wicked knife sheathed in Tennessee rattlesnake on his belt. A jolly type, he buys a Budweiser and gator samplers for complete strangers. It turns out that he, too, is a German, once a police officer in Hamburg. He and Jesse, the restaurant proprietor, are old pals. A Cuban woman hurries from Sally's deep-fry kitchen with a plate of the freshest frogs' legs available. "Come to Coopertown, ya'll, and get something besides beef and pork," Jesse, the Missourian still, says.

Gator Bill loads tourists on an airboat to take pictures of gators.

Biker Jens holds the head from a twelve-foot gator in front of Coopertown Restaurant.

This is America at her best, especially when it comes to eating. It is a good-humored place, most of the time. You can amble over to the locally famous Coopertown Bridge across U.S. 41, better known as the Tamiami Trail, but run for your life if those infernal Yankees, Canucks, or Cubans are bearing down on you in full daylight with their headlights on. They drive faster when their lights are on, and in daylight the beams *obscure* what they're approaching. This cross-state artery has perhaps the most bountiful road kill in the world. Once on the rickety wooden bridge, slow down like a family of otters and sniff the fresh air. This bridge should be renamed in honor of the waitress Ellen Curtis, who sat on it for ten days so that some fool government guys wouldn't blow it up. Ellen is still around, although now on crutches, and she will explain to you why she saved the bridge.

Next to three boys fishing with cane poles by the lock on the other side of Ellen's shaky bridge, I look into the puffy cumulus over the Everglades and see the British Concorde riding low on her landing approach. I tell the boys. They get very excited, but get even more excited when the pygmy rattlesnake crawls out of the banana grove.

In the white heat of high noon Jesse Kennon, wearing cowpoke duds and no hat, kneels in the sun by his huge new airboat. The waitress who sat on the bridge and preserved it trundles by on her crutches. Jesse is weary: he did most of the labor on the restaurant's new roof, bathrooms, and exterior himself. The telephone rings inside the Coopertown restaurant. "Jeee-see. Jeee-see," a voice calls.

Like a wounded fox, Jesse Kennon slouches toward the telephone. "That damn phone follows me!" Minutes later, he emerges with a grin. "We got two busloads of Germans, and a French movie crew made reservations for breakfast tomorrow." Jesse celebrates with a Dr. Pepper. If this were Mudville, he might be Ol' Casey at the plate.

> *When it comes to eating, this is America at her best. It is a good-humored place, most of the time.*

Some time if you're in Coopertown, when Jesse isn't too busy, ask him to show you the big Coopertown scrapbook with the snapshots of gators, sunsets, airboats, and Mariel Hemingway showing her breasts. Take a stroll from the Coopertown Restaurant to the adjacent bait shop over in front of the cackleberry patch and puppy-pens. Blond Ned, the owner, looks as if he comes from Hanover, but he's really from Kendall, a Miami suburb. Once Mariel Hemingway made a movie here, and Ned got to meet her. That's one of the real advantages of Coopertown. Why, you might run into Helmut Newton, Chuck Norris, or Margaret Trudeau out here. Don't forget that the critters are more important than the folks, though. For example, never, ever mess with a baby gator even if you like his or her chirp and cute face. They just don't do well in Toronto.

Ned imports large worms from Canada. He has lots of Polaroids on the wall of fishermen holding bass and bream, and hunters holding up the heads of deer and gators. He also always has an up-to-date supply of official state of Florida fish and game rules and maps, free of charge. The Florida Highway Patrol squad car parks at Ned's. Like Jesse, Ned has all the American beers, but he also has the cold grape soda you can't get next door.

At the restaurant, study that large faded portrait on the wall of the craggy, kind-faced man wearing a hat and a 12-gauge with the barrel barely showing. That's the mayor, Big John Cooper. He has gone to meet his Maker, but he's still mayor. Big John was from Missouri, and his military service in the Second World War required no stripes or bars. Big John worked in an ammo plant. It was the best money he ever made, and he put some of it away. When he returned to rural Missouri after the new-fangled bombs ended the big war, why it looked like Missouri itself had been bombed by B-29s. Big John did what any man who loves life would do: he got the hell out, even though he would always call Missouri home.

He moved south to SW 8th Street in Miami. He invented the airboat. Breakfast was his favorite meal, never with frogs, and he knew the Everglades as well as the celebrated Tiger family of Seminoles, really Miccosukees, who were his neighbors. Oh, Big John is dead, but he is not buried. Where will his ashes be scattered—the boot heel of Missouri or the swamp called the Everglades? They sell an old postcard for twenty-five cents in the Coopertown Restaurant. Look closely—that's Big John driving the craft. So Coopertown affirms, in every bite of frogs' legs and in the old Florida postcards, that there is something to this from-here-to-eternity business. Counterpoint to the road kill.

In wintertime (Florida has only two seasons: summer and February), the sunsets out here will take your breath away. Jesse is a sunset specialist. He can tell you hours ahead of time whether there will be a good one. The sunsets of Coopertown pale the celebrated ones at Key West. And they'll make you hunger for some of the deep-fried vittles from Sally's kitchen. If you're reading this in a Miami Beach hotel room, call Sally at 226-6048, and she'll have a hot plate ready for you when you get to Coopertown, the last place in the Miami phone book that lists SW 8th Street as its address.

GATOR RECIPES

Winning recipes from Gatorland's Great Gator Cook-Off in Orlando.

GATOR GOULASH

1 ounce double-smoked bacon, diced
2 tablespoons olive oil
12 ounces alligator tenderloin, thinly sliced
1 ounce andouille sausage
2 ounces onion, finely diced
2 ounces garlic, chopped
1 green and 1 red pepper, sliced
1 tomato, peeled and pureéd
rosemary, thyme, and oregano, chopped, to taste
½ cup white wine
cracked black peppercorns, salt, cayenne pepper, to taste
parsley, chopped
chives, chopped
saffron rice

In a hot skillet, cook bacon in olive oil until it browns slightly. Add alligator and sausage and cook until just done, a few minutes. Then add onion and garlic and sauté until onion is transparent. Add peppers, tomato, herbs, and white wine. Reduce liquid until it has a full, rich flavor. Season with peppercorns, salt, and cayenne. Garnish with parsley and chives; serve over saffron rice. *Serves four.*

GATOR SCALLOPINI WITH SUN-DRIED PEACH AND BRANDY SAUCE

6 ounces alligator meat
1 cup milk
1 cup lime juice
4 eggs
1 cup pecans, crushed
oil for sautéing
4 ounces brandy
1 tablespoon brown sugar
2 ounces raspberry vinegar
½ tablespoon shallots
4 ounces orange juice
½ tablespoon jalapeño peppers, chopped
3 ounces sun-dried peaches, diced
2 ounces unsalted butter

Pound alligator meat between two sheets of waxed paper to a uniform thickness of ⅛ inch. Cover with milk and lime juice and soak for two days, refrigerated. Crack eggs into marinade, then remove meat and shake off excess. Dust with crushed pecans. Sauté, two minutes each side, in oil Remove to a heated plate. Drain excess oil from pan and·deglaze with brandy. Light to burn off the alcohol. Add brown sugar, raspberry vinegar, shallots, orange juice, and jalapeño peppers and bring to a boil. Add sun-dried peaches and salt and pepper to taste. Reduce mixture by one-third. Whisk in butter, pour sauce over alligator meat, and serve. *Serves two.*

GATOR RIBS

1 pound gator ribs
MARINADE:
2 12-ounce cans beer
3/4 cup soy sauce
1 cup Italian salad dressing
2 tablespoons lemon-pepper seasoning
juice of 2 lemons
2 dashes Crystal Hot Sauce
1 dash red wine vinegar
salt and pepper, to taste
BARBEQUE SAUCE
½ gallon Cattleman, or your favorite BBQ sauce
1 cup Worcestershire sauce
2 tablespoons cayenne pepper
1 ounce Crystal Hot Sauce

Mix all marinade ingredients together in a large bowl. Put ribs in a shallow pan and marinate for 12 to 24 hours, refrigerated. Pour off marinade, leaving a little in the pan. Bake the ribs in the pan, covered, 30 to 45 minutes, at 325 degrees. Mix together BBQ sauce ingredients. Remove ribs from oven, put in clean pan, and cover with BBQ sauce. Grill to your liking. *Serves four.*

BURRGATA PICCATA

2 pounds alligator meat
salt and pepper
flour
3 tablespoons butter
1 tablespoon olive oil
2 cloves garlic, chopped
½ pound mushrooms, sliced
juice of ½ lemon
2 tablespoons capers, in juice
¾ cup white wine
parsley
½ lemon, thinly sliced

Use the "catfish" tenderloin of the tail or the jaw of the alligator for best results. Pound the alligator meat to ¼-inch thickness. Sprinkle with salt and pepper and dust lightly with flour on both sides. Heat butter and olive oil in large skillet. Add gator and brown on both sides. Remove and keep warm. Add garlic and mushrooms to pan and sauté, then add browned meat. Add lemon juice, capers, caper juice, and wine. Cover and simmer 20 minutes. Place alligator meat on a warm platter and cover with juice and capers from pan. Garnish with parsley and twisted lemon slices. Excellent served with long grain and wild rice and broccoli. *Serves six.*

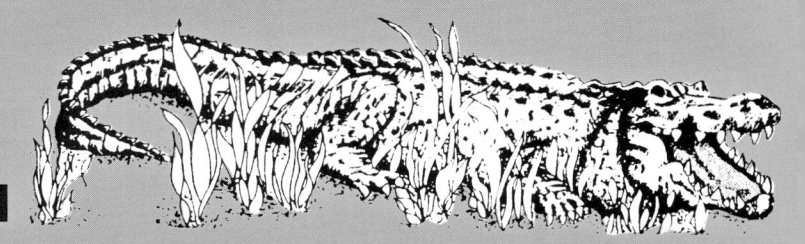

Secured by an underwater cord, a gator swims toward the film crew on cue.

A big gator can grab a hundred-pound hog
and crush its head like a potato chip,
spraying brains twenty-five feet.

—ED FROEHLICH
Gator farmer

*Actors in Austrian soft drink ad
filmed in the Glades.*

CHAPTER 3

NOT THE BLUE DANUBE

Gator farmer Ed Froehlich knows gators, and knows that a big gator, like a big anything, should be treated with some respect.

In the alligator's case this is especially true when it is in the water.

Swilling Löwenbräu and swatting skeeters at the site of the annual wild hog barbeque in Collier County, I watch Jesse Kennon save a couple of Banana Republic–outfitted Europeans from one of the worst fates imaginable, something like Mr. Froehlich's hog brains tale. South Florida at the time is crawling with Austrians, something to do with weather, schilling exchange rates, and this wonderland named by the Spanish for flowers. These particular ones are doing a TV spot in the Glades for a Viennese soft drink.

A milk-fed, auburn-tressed *Mädchen* from the Alps, her breasts partially visible when she kneels by the muck to take a snapshot of a trussed six-foot female gator, is to be rescued from other, untrussed, hungry gators by a cowboy with an earring. Once saved, she is to sip the Austrian soft drink with the cowboy while the cameras roll. The cowboy, a Scots-Berliner, was once a soldier in Belfast.

Accordingly, Jesse and the Miccosukee Gator King, Bobby Tiger, turn an eight-foot bull gator loose in the mire, holding it by a green plastic cord under the water. The khaki-clad assistant director and his aide, shooting with a $100,000 35mm movie camera, demand more drama. Now, gators aren't all that dramatic on cue, so an exciter is used, as in billfishing, except this one isn't plastic, but a store-bought chicken.

Instead of showing any interest in the chicken, however, the gator does the unexpected: he dives below the surface and heads towards the camera crew standing waist high in Everglades water.

Jesse moves quickly into the water to find the gator and the green safety cord, while the camera crew starts to save themselves and their equipment. Shortly Jesse, in wet cowboy shirt and jeans, has the gator under control, and the commercial is completed without further drama. It will doubtlessly attract many more Europeans to Florida, home of the alligator.

The Austrians later leave for Epcot. "So much for the gator," says the woman from Wien, now wearing a leopard-skin top.

Bobby Tiger and Jesse get gator in position for filming.

Dennis and Lynn bring in the first gator of the night.

CHAPTER 4

THE SWAMP BUGGY KING

Leonard Chessner, forty-eight, is the revered Cracker king of swamp buggy racers in Naples on the Gulf Coast. His entry in 1988 is more advanced than a Stealth bomber. His wife, Lynn, a registered nurse and a paramedic, is a beautiful woman for these woods. They have graciously invited Richard and me to accompany them on the hunt for their eleventh gator in a spooky foray that begins off Alligator Alley, exactly where the state Game and Fish boys started the big gator hunt earlier in the month.

We ride with Leonard in a glitzy ninety-horsepower bass boat named Wildfire XVII. Lynn and her twenty-seven-year-old son from a previous marriage, Dennis Hoolihan, take off first in a Jonboat, a low-slung Florida swamper boat particularly good for taking gators. She is wearing a Bo hat and a Chola red top and looks more as if she should be at Miami's Mayfair, a swank hotel and shopping complex where the Chessners and their friends do spend some weekends. Lynn, Leonard, and Dennis call each other "Ma" and "Pa" and "Punkin" on the CB radios.

The family is Irish and a pioneer one in Collier County, exactly to the west of Miami across the Everglades. With a Hoolihan and a Mahoney on this hunt, something is bound to happen. The Chessners have been hunting these swamps since just after the Civil War. Leonard knew his grandpap and his great grandad at advanced ages. With the help of their experience and lore, he has been a trapper since age fifteen. Before this warm Florida night, the present-day Chessner clan has harvested 97 feet of alligators—ten of them—the largest 11.7 feet. Tonight is Lynn's turn, and you can sense the excitement in her. She is from a town in Ohio, where every Halloween the embalmed body of a man named Eugene, kept on display year-round as a

Leonard with an iced gator from the night's hunt.

good example of a local funeral home's fine work, mysteriously appears on the City Hall steps or propped upright on a Yankee infantryman's statue. So there are stranger places than these Glades.

The Chessners have built their own harpoons and are well larded for the expedition. Lynn has made ham sandwiches with slices of onion, and there are plenty of Pepsis and Budweiser.

The canals are wide and we are completely alone. Leonard, a good ole boy in a B.A.S.S. Association baseball cap, jokes and slightly guns the powerful boat under the Alligator Alley overpass. Mother and son have disappeared. The sun sets over the Gulf of Mexico. I spread more Miracle Whip on my sandwich with my big knife and pop open a Bud. Leonard jumps as if someone is shooting at him.

"Sh-h-h," he cautions, slapping about a hundred skeeters

Lynn carefully soaps and washes down a gator prior to skinning.

Leonard and Dennis skin a gator, taking special care not to damage the hide.

with his hand. "If we're going to kill him, we can't talk or make noises with beer cans." Darkness falls and a lovely crescent moon begins to climb. There is heat lightning to the north, the same bursts to the south, and Leonard can't help but talk low.

"I used to do a lot of gator cave hunting in the summertime around Immokalee. I'd pull 'em out through the holes with my bare hands. You grab the gator by the big bone in his head, and he twists and fights hard. On hard ground, they're dangerous. So you shoot the gator in the eye and the ear, cut his backbone, and run a strong reed through it so it won't wiggle like a rattlesnake does until sundown, when you cut off its head."

The bass boat drifts to the saw grass of the canalside. The moon is down fast. The mosquito spray does not work. We hear crackling on the radio from Lynn: "Hey, Punkin . . ."

"Yes, dear," Leonard replies. "We're going to have to sit here," says Lynn, "and wait for the big ol' gator to settle."

The radios, ham-and-onion sandwiches, and everything else is forgotten. From the bushes behind our boat, something massive is crashing through the reeds straight for us. Is it a fugitive, a water buffalo as in Vietnam, a runaway airboat? The three of us duck as it sails through the air and hits the water near our outboard. It's a gator, ten feet at least and moving like a racehorse until he hits the canal, where he settles down, his grinning head above water.

We are all thrilled, especially Leonard. He starts talking to it.

"Umph," he says.

"Umph," says the gator.

"Umph," replies Leonard.

It sort of sounds like a person who needs a meal, the universal noise of a hungry stomach.

The big fellow is wary and soon submerges for good. Leonard puts on his coal miner's light hat and begins to slowly propel the boat with a foot pedal from the front, umphing all the way. The big one is gone, but Leonard manages to pull a baby gator from the bushes to show us. Damn if the little feller doesn't go "u-umph."

The radio crackles again. "Pop, have you got your ears on?"

Lynn and her boy Dennis are headed toward us. The big one they were seeking has escaped the harpoon and is probably in a cave. Suddenly, their lights pick up the red eyes of a target near us. Leonard again warns against pop tops and talking. It's a kill.

With the moon down, we are in total darkness. The Jonboat advances. There is a splashing as the snare and harpoon fly toward the prey. Frantic tugging and cursing from the Jonboat. We pull alongside. Leonard is critical of the way Dennis used the harpoon. The gator goes almost seven feet in length, a disappointing size. Dennis takes an axe and whacks its neck.

Lynn goes to check the sex of the capture because she had fouled up on that in a previous kill; the state wildlife boys want to know the sex of each kill. She is eloquent there in the bloody Everglades: "Now we see if it is dead or alive."

Sexing alligators is not easy under high-intensity lights in laboratories. At night in the Everglades, the male member can actually wound you. Lynn leans in the Jonboat while her son holds up the weighty tail so that she can get to the cloaca, a slit inside which the sexual organs are contained. She slides two fingers into the slit, cool and mushy. "There's nothing big in there," she reports, as a

After nearly two hours of skinning, the soft, smooth hide is removed.

musk fills the air. "Female for sure."

Sexing gators is no easy job. All that scientists know about gator sex itself is that crocodilians have short bouts of copulation—up to three minutes and usually underwater. There is no muscular ejaculation in the male, and there is no knowledge whether an orgasm occurs. If gator sex is still a secret, we are about to learn that gator violence and power are certainly as the tales say.

"Emergency," the radio barks. "Pa, help us. Help us!"

Sexing gators is no easy job.

Leonard goes full speed, and it is all I can do to hold on. The Everglades suddenly become a ninety-thousand horse-power carnival ride.

Pulling into a canal choked with swamp lettuce and other water plants, we find the Jonboat rocking, Dennis soaked, the harpoon and its orange float missing, and Lynn crying, "Pa! Pa! Pa!"

Their night had almost been made. They had closed on a huge bull gator lying on the surface. Dennis had hurled the harpoon and before the eyes of his mother was pulled into the black water with the twisting, wounded beast. The young man had nearly turned the Jonboat over as he scrambled for life. While Lynn wails, Leonard begins a determined hunt for the gator with the harpoon and the orange float in its back.

"Umph," Leonard calls, over and over.

The bass boat gets stuck momentarily in the swamp lettuce, and I am sure at that moment that I smell very angry alligator musk. Hallucinatory orange floats and wounded bulls appear in the water and the brush. A pair of deer watch our strange actions from a levee path. The stars shift a whole lot, and suddenly a pair of red eyes confronts us.

It isn't him, but a five-footer still carrying his youth's markings. I stand in the back of the bass boat and nearly make Leonard jump into the water by popping another Bud. "God, that gator is beautiful," I think. "What a beautiful swimmer and how motionless he can hang." The little alligator peels away from us and disappears in an instant. For an unknown reason, here in the nadir of the black dawn hunt for the harpooned bull, I stand up in the bass boat and pop yet another Bud. Leonard's eyes exude sweat under the miner's light he is so angry. If he weren't a gentleman hunter, Leonard would probably have harpooned me, he is so pissed.

Before dawn, Leonard and Lynn give up the search. At morning's light, the orange float and the gator are found by another hunter. Lynn cooks a big breakfast in the Naples compound, some gator skinning is done, and a German journalist from *Stern* magazine calls to ask if she could go out with the Chessners. I tell her over the telephone that Leonard and Lynn are what we Floridians call good folks. Certainly, they are. Later, she flies down from Seattle and is introduced to ham, Miracle Whip, and onion sandwiches.

Even later, after I relate the tale in Naples of the son in the water with the enraged bull before his mother's eyes, a Cracker slaps his knee and exclaims: "Whoo-ee, if that had been me in the water with that 'un, I'd've come back into the Jonboat dry as a pig's whistle I would've got out of that water so fast." Dennis, to his credit, never seemed to have any embarrassment about the incident.

Dennis, Lynn, and Leonard with skinned gators.

Rejoice, O young man in thy youth.

—ECCLESIASTES

CHAPTER 5

NUBS: A BOY'S GATOR

Gators, like people, have distinctive personalities. Often it comes from some physical aberration, such as the mother alligator up in the Okeefenokee on the Georgia line who had her eyes poked out but went on successfully to raise a nest of hatchlings. Was she a biological computer or was it gator mother love? I know that I once had a gator that I loved, loved that little devil like a dog, although, admittedly, gators don't return affection. His name was Nubs, and he was three feet long and had only three feet. A fisherman in the Dead Lakes near Wewahitchka had snagged him and axed his right rear leg in trying to untangle the little fellow from his line.

Through some childhood miracle, a neighbor who was out for shellcracker, warmouth, and bream in the very alive Dead Lakes brought it home to me in a tin tub. Pig Heilig, a hulking construction worker from Alabama who lived in a big trailer behind our house, gave Nubs to me, a gift of no small magnitude to a thirteen-year-old in the panhandle town of Panama City, already deep into motorcycles, guns, and bay boats.

Nubs showed no visible pain from his amputation and promptly bit both me and Pig. I kept him in a little swimming pool my uncle had built in the pines and fed him, along with toads and turtles, my brother's chickens and table scraps.

Nubs was aggressive, perhaps more so because of his missing foot. At night, with the cicadas humming in the pines, I would shine a flashlight into the pool and he would charge the light, all but climbing out of his concrete prison. His were the first red gator eyes I ever saw.

The stump healed right up. One day I decided to take him to biology class, securing him in the same tub in which Pig Heilig had brought him to me. I put him on the back of my Harley-Davidson and proudly drove off to junior high with a creature whose sixty-foot ancestors had lived with dinosaurs during the Mesozoic Era over 230 million years ago.

I never even got the chance to show and tell. The girls squealed at the motorcyclist with the reptile in the tub. Nubs snapped more than usual. The three-footer did not cotton to school, and the principal sent me home after Nubs bit me once again. I spent the day—a gator holiday—with him by the pool, killed a chicken for him, and wondered about his stump, if gators feel pain.

In three months, my pet gator was gone in the night. I like to think of him now as a twelve-footer in some Panama City bayou and that maybe some of the local fishermen call him Ol' Three Legs or something. When I used to hear Linda Ronstadt sing "Blue Bayou," I would think not of junior high girlfriends, but of Nubs and the kindly Alabama construction man named Pig who brought a boy a special living gift from the Dead Lakes.

Every boy should have a Nubs.

CHAPTER 6

THE OLD MAN AND THE LAKE

And a thousand slimy things

Lived on; and so did I.

—SAMUEL COLERIDGE
The Rime of the Ancient Mariner

Columbus H. White of C. H. White Meats, Inc., in the hamlet of Lochloosa in Florida's lake country, is a famous and esteemed man in the region. White, sixty-three, wearing overalls and a baseball cap, leans back in the swing in his front yard filled with blonde urchins and dogs and gently and forthrightly tells how he killed the biggest gator of all in 1989. As a professor said at the nearby University of Florida, "That was some animal."

Despite his fame and success as a trapper and meat processor, White is a sad and troubled man with a son, only thirty-seven, who was maimed in a collision with a pulpwood truck and later developed heart trouble. Columbus finds it hard to stay off the subject of his son, Danny, sitting in the heat of the afternoon next to two live gators swimming in a tank and a freezer containing icy alligator heads. But as he talks about the Big One, a touch of excitement enters his Alabama-Florida drawl. "It took us four months to find him and kill him," says the old man, who came to these lakes from Wetumpka, Alabama, at the age of seven and has traveled the world.

Fame? Everybody from Ocala to Gainesville to Palatka knows about Trapper White. He just made Paul Harvey's radio show for getting the Big One, which went 1,043 pounds, wouldn't fit in the cooler, and dwarfed the red pickup truck they finally brought him to town in. "But you know I missed the radio show," he says of his moment of media glory. "I didn't hear myself on Paul Harvey, but I was there."

Trapper White, even in his backwoods setting, is a man astute on Florida wildlife, politics, and the Audubon Society. He saw the world courtesy of the United States Navy as an early recruit in World War II, before he started his war against gators.

He relishes his Navy years like only a Southern veteran can. After boot camp, he served as a seaman and gunner on merchant marine ships under navy command. He went up the Seine in France and remembers eating pumpkins and watermelons at the Pyramids in Egypt. He was in Sydney, Australia, when the war ended, preparing for the invasion of Japan. His ship did go to Japan, half loaded with beer. "I knew a real good Christian sailor who picked up a Jap head full of that there radiation," White said, "The sailor said he was going to take the head home to his girlfriend, but the man died of radiation sickness."

The wind from the lake scrapes the moss and twigs on

the tin roof of the house that Columbus White built himself in 1946 after returning from Hiroshima. White blinks his blue eyes and returns to 1989 and the killing of what he calls a "problem gator," rather than using the wildlife officers' term "nuisance gator." Actually, the thing was not a nuisance, just big and scary and a potential threat to the poodles and little kids who walk out on the docks of the private fishing camp on weed-choked Orange Lake. "I don't know how old he was," White says, "anywhere from thirty to a hundred, and he had got big and bold by eating all those fish heads and guts at the camp."

The hunt required four expeditions in its four months. The night of the kill was long and eerie.

"My son, despite his sickness and handicap, drove the airboat. At first we couldn't find the critter anywhere, then he surfaced but just for a second. Then the gator disappeared in a tussock or floating island of myrtle trees. We sent the harpoons in after him, floating jugs attached to them as spotters. Before long we had two harpoons in him under that tussock. He fought but we pulled him out with the airboat. Somebody said in the night, 'I don't know how big he is, but he's big.'" The Orange Lake night was broken with the hissing, thrashing tumult of man against reptile. The reptile really never stood much of a chance.

"It took us three and a half hours to winch his head aboard the airboat. From nine to way past midnight and into the dawn, which is mighty black out on the lake. Yeah, we were scared and we were working hard. I was worried about Danny up there in the captain's seat. When we got the gator's head out of the water we were amazed at the size. And the harpoons and the jugs were floating out in the blackwater."

The old man of the lake pauses and wipes the sweat of

the July evening from under the baseball cap. A gator inside the tank knocks against the tin.

"Finally, that big old head was grinning at us in the airboat. I shot him with a .357 Magnum between the eyes. The first time killed him, but then I fired another to make sure."

The word spread quickly to the state government of what Columbus White had done. Local folks got a look at the awesome carcass before it was put into brine, then butchered. The 1,043-pound denizen was 13.10 feet long. Over in Apalachicola, a lighter but longer gator was captured, but Columbus claims his was a few inches more if you measured the old full-nose-bend way. Weeks later, newspapers carried small reports of the great catch. A Louisiana broker bought the hide.

Columbus is philosophical about it. He has a missing finger from the attack of a smaller and more dangerous gator, an attack that sent accompanying wildlife officers

Forty miles southwest of Atlanta, Georgia, Griffin is home to one of the biggest gator and exotic leather tanners.

Taxidermist Ken Jordan of Fort Drum displaying his recently completed gator heads.

scattering for safety. He uses the familiar line: "There ain't no such thing as a dead gator." The clouds return to the trapper's eyes. Is it his son who so pulls at his heart? Is it the sailor and the radioactive head?

And that's the full story of glory, such as it is, Paul Harvey.

Skin from Columbus H. White's big gator at tanner in Griffin.

"That big old head was grinning at us in the airboat.
I shot him between the eyes with my .357 Magnum.
The first time killed him, then I fired another
to make sure."

CHAPTER 7

THE TIGER VS. THE LEVIATHAN

Bobby Tiger, Miccosukee, is one of Florida's truly distinguished citizens. A Miccosukee is a member of the secessionist tribe that

in 1948 broke away from the famous Seminoles. The Miccosukee flag that flutters over the palm-thatched villages along Tamiami Trail is almost a duplicate of the German colors. The Tiger family has always been prominent in the tribe, but soft-spoken Bobby says of his father, "He was just an ordinary man." Bobby's mother gave birth to him in the Everglades brush west of Miami, in a place with no name. The boy's first name was Aleemahstchee, untranslatable from something to do with pineapples and a lizard's end. The Miccosukee boys wore skirts like their sisters, but learned to hunt early, without guns. Gators were everywhere and were respected not only for their fierceness but especially for the size they attained.

When he was a teenager, Bobby walked into Miami one night and enrolled in English classes at the night school of Miami Senior High. Soon, at fifteen, he wrestled his first

Special Florida license plate for Miccosukee tribe members.

For more than fifty years, Bobby Tiger has shown tourists what he learned in the Glades: respect for alligators and how to wrestle them.

A recently arrived wrestling gator. Bobby's pole gives him some protection from the gator's tail and jaws should it attack.

gator at the tourist attraction, now long gone, called Musa Isle, on the bank of the Miami River. A high-rise now takes the place where real Indians once displayed their way of life to northern tourists.

In the Asian way of American Indians, Tiger seems ageless and fearless, and the show still goes on a half century after Musa Isle. Early in his career, in 1948, the handsome young Indian was flown by Pan Am to Nassau, where he rassled a gator at a very charming pink British hotel. He travels now mainly in a red pickup truck with a special Indian license plate.

Bobby, wise in the ways of gator reproduction and life in the wild, is eloquent on the subjects of Indian diet and health, Everglades animism, and American Indian politics. He dresses in a distinguished blue short-sleeved jacket generally called a Seminole top.

At the Wild Hog Barbecue and Jamboree held off the Tamiami Trail near Monroe Station, deep in the Glades, Bobby is working with a dangerous eight-footer. The gator hisses; the people gasp. The temperature feels like 110 degrees, and a child notices that Bobby is missing a finger.

Call him "Mister Bobby Tiger, *Professional* Miccosukee Indian Alligator Wrestler," because there was a time when he put shows on in certain Miami Beach hotels and was called boy and swindled out of his fee after sticking his head inside the mouth of a mean bull gator.

So professionalism comes to the Glades. The grand old man of gatordom has appeared in many movies, among them *Joe Panther* (1976), *Bank of the Hand* (1987), and the classic *Shark River* (1957). He trained the current alligator act in the Ringling Bros., Barnum & Bailey circus.

Bobby performs his show at Holiday Park near Alligator Alley. In his younger days, Bobby would put his head into the jaws of large bull gators.

Bobby charms the staff at Flamingo Gardens.

Gator wrestling for students on a field trip to Flamingo Gardens.

Gator wrestling. It's a subject you'll never be able to take as an elective at Miami Senior High. There is a lot of responsibility—red tape, if you will. You can't just go out to a swamp, drag a gator out by his tail, kill the critter in the back of a pickup truck, or keep it alive for the show.

Rule Number One in Florida: It is against the law to capture alligators from the wild. Bobby, even though he is a native-born Indian living in the Everglades, still has to apply to the state of Florida for special permits and licenses to transport his gators and put on gator wrestling shows. Bobby has custom-made aluminum shipping crates to carry his gators, both in his pickup and on the airlines when he travels out of state. The basic bottom line is to respect the gator—small or large.

These days, as European tourists file out of silver air-conditioned buses at Holiday Park at the western fringes

of Fort Lauderdale to ride airboats into the Glades and see gators, Bobby still puts on seven shows a day.

At night the old man of the Everglades, once a barefoot boy in a skirt, travels alone across the Glades. Alone except for his legal gators in the back of the truck.

Rule Number One in Florida:
It is against the law
to capture alligators from the wild.

CHAPTER 8

THE TOWN
NAMED FOR THE ALLIGATOR

*Around the turn of the century,
in the beginning of the Miami dream, the gator-rich Biscayne Prairie
became more popular than the piney woods of the bayside.*

"Allapattah" is a name that rolls easily off the tongue. In Seminole, it means that most fierce of Florida critters: alligator. As a

district of Miami away from the bay, Allapattah's story has largely been neglected. But there's always been a frontier spirit about the place. It grew up on true grit. Here is a historic tapestry that tells the Allapattah story.

Pineapples. Papayas. Papaya honey. In the beginning of the Miami dream, around the turn of the century, the gator-rich Biscayne Prairie became more popular than the piney woods of the bayside. These flatlands between the bay and the Everglades had strange names: Humbuggus, Pocomoonshine, Allapattah. "Julia Tuttle (founder of Miami) must have fallen in love with the Biscayne Prairie the first time she saw it sweeping out of the distant northwest like a broad, grassy river, offering a hint of the still mysterious Everglades," says Thelma Peters of Biscayne Country. People of European and African descent began to realize the agricultural riches of the prairie. One such family was that of Captain Stephen Andrews, who moved west from Lemon City to farm. These "truckers," as they became known, were from all over the world: Andrews from Canterbury, England, and others from Bremen, Nassau, Shanghai, Savannah, and elsewhere.

NW 36th Street, still the main street of Allapattah, was a dirt trail in 1898. That's the year that a German immigrant, Louis J. Becker, known as Old Man Becker, donated land for a schoolhouse, which his neighbors built with their own hands. There were fourteen pupils at first. At the beginning, one teacher rode her bicycle on paths through palmetto wilderness to get there each day. Old Man Becker's single-room schoolhouse became Miami Jackson High School, one of the three oldest in the city. Named for Andrew Jackson, the feisty Tennessee general who later became one of the best United States presidents after serving as Florida's first territorial governor, Jackson High has always played a large role in Allapattah life. Its athletic teams are, of course, called the Generals instead of the Gators. Many Generals have gone on to play professional ball, including Michael Thompson, who plays basketball for the Los Angeles Lakers. The motto of Jackson, whose colors are green and gold, is "The School that Cares."

"Alligator" is one of Miami's oldest communities. Today it is loosely bound by I-95, the Airport Expressway (112),

the Miami River to the south, and the Miami jai alai fronton at its western tip. A population approaching 60,000 exceeds that of Little Havana (50,000), Coconut Grove (23,000), and many other well-known Dade County cities and neighborhoods. Miami city officials say that Allapattah is 75 percent Latin, 10 percent African American, and 15 percent white.

The Allapatah district is trying hard for a comeback. There are Allapattah bumper stickers with gators on them. NW 36th Street and other Allapattah arteries are being revitalized. Because those who know the area and its history love the place, there is a good chance for economic and social rebirth.

They named this place
for what we Cubans call **El Lagarto.**

—RAY FLEITES
Cuban banker

Allapattah has always been a good example of ingenuity. There was the Old Hen Hotel on NW 27th Avenue and NW 34th Street. It was a huge unfinished structure that was started as a hotel for people during the boom year of 1925. The hurricane of 1926 did not blow the building away, but it did blow away the hope for a hotel. Instead, the structure became a hatchery containing 60,000 laying hens, 50,000 fryers, and 50,000 incubator chicks. A promoter came up with a name for the place: The Million Dollar Hen Hotel. Someone should come up with a Million Dollar Alligator Farm Hotel.

Allapattah today no longer has a Hen Hotel, but it does have the Miami baseball stadium, the city's Farmers Market, the previously mentioned and distinguished Jackson High School, the Civic Center Hospitals, Round Towers, Curtis Park, and the oldest, biggest jai alai fronton in the hemisphere. At a little museum in nearby Arch Creek are photographs of giant gators and crocodiles killed by hunters at the turn of the century. But there are no alligators today in Allapattah.

University of Florida Gator Tiffany Coyle.

CHAPTER 9

THE NATURE OF THE CREATURE

Behold him rushing forth from the flags and reeds.
His enormous body swells. His plaited tail brandished high, floats upon the lake.
The waters like a cataract descend from his opening jaws. Clouds of smoke issue
from his dilated nostrils....

—WILLIAM BARTRAM
Travels, 1791

So wrote the Quaker naturalist and explorer after an extensive tour of east and west Florida, Georgia, and the Carolinas in 1791. What was Bartram describing? It was the alligator—the modern dragon—a creature that brings Florida to mind every bit as much as do palm trees, Spanish moss, and oranges. Bartram was one of the first to write of the alligator, and if his observations are more romantic than accurate, they do reflect the fascination centered about this beast that continues

How dangerous are alligators?
Some say gators are vicious, with a constant desire
to clamp their traplike jaws on human or beast.
Others maintain they are basically peaceable reptiles,
more interested in snoozing than biting and will attack
only when provoked.

down to today.

For visitors and native Floridians alike, it's still an awesome experience to see a big gator basking on a sun-baked highway. And alligator farms are big tourist attractions at St. Augustine, Orlando, and Silver Springs, with dozens of smaller ones scattered throughout the state. There are still a few easily accessible places—Everglades National Park in south Florida and Wakulla Springs in the Big Bend, to cite two—where alligators can be viewed in their natural habitat.

Spanish explorers probing their way about in the New World encountered large numbers of the big reptiles. To them, alligators were the "terrible lizards." It was from the Spanish *el lagarto* that the English coined the word "alligator."

Bartram wrote of commonly coming upon alligators up to twenty feet long. Just how big gators do grow has been a hot subject of debate for three centuries. Back in Bartram's day, alligators probably grew larger than they do in present-day Florida because of a lack of natural enemies. But substantive figures in the record books don't support the many tales about twenty-footers. A nineteen-foot, two-inch specimen killed by the father of Louisiana naturalist E. A. McIlhenny was the biggest that can be verified without question. Monster gators in the fifteen- to sixteen-foot class have been killed at infrequent times since the turn of the century, and a seventeen-footer was reported taken in the 1959–1960 hunting season. Big George, the center of attraction at Ross Allen's Reptile Institute in Silver Springs, is the largest specimen in captivity today, at fourteen feet, seven inches. In 1957, the U. S. Fish and Wildlife Service said that twelve feet was regarded as the alligator maximum in the United States, although fifteen-footers were not unusual fifty years ago.

Gators are quite social as they take their daily sun.

How dangerous are alligators? This, like the question of size, is a point of dispute. Some say gators are vicious, with a constant desire to clamp their traplike jaws on human or beast. Others maintain that they are basically peaceable reptiles, more interested in snoozing than biting, and will attack only when provoked, like most other animals.

Dr. Earle Frye, assistant director of the Florida Game and Fresh Water Fish Commission, says that one thing is fairly clear about the question of danger: Alligators are most likely to develop bold and aggressive personalities as they grow larger and are unmolested by humans. Then, Frye says, the gator may attack dogs, cattle, and even humans.

Often an attempt by an alligator to get away from a human who has stumbled upon it in a swamp or some body of water is mistakenly termed an attack. And, like any other animal, a female gator will attack if her nest or young are disturbed.

Some unthinking people have been injured by alligators because of stupid pranks. For example, in 1958 a Tampa man happened to come upon a twelve-footer stretched out on a highway and for some reason grabbed it by its tail. Fortunately, a few deep gashes on the man's right leg were all that the surprised gator managed to inflict.

Gators have always provided a rich source of folklore in Florida, and some of the stories are hard to match. For example, take the following one, from Richard Bothwell's book, *Alligators:*

"Camped on the shores of a large pond near Tampa many years ago, Joe Culbreath decided to do a little night fishing, although the rest of his party was busy fighting mosquitoes.

"He stripped off his clothing except a vest and his derby. The vest was necessary to carry his cigars, matches, and bacon rind baits. The band of the derby carried his extra hooks. He walked out into that dark pond until the water came up just beyond his vest.

"On the bottom, Joe felt what he thought was a log with rough bark. He stood on it and began casting. A big fish was hooked and as he was pulling it in the 'log' began moving—he stood atop a big alligator which had seen the struggling fish and decided to dine.

"Things happened fast. The alligator took after the fish, with Joe atop the gator's back. The fish made for the opposite shore and jumped from the water to dry land. Joe was knocked off the alligator's back by the limb of an overhanging tree. But he waded ashore and secured the fish, which he exhibited to the party as evidence of his adventure."

FARMING THE GATOR

There are about fifty alligator farms in Florida and Louisiana raising gators for meat and hides. Many double as tourist attractions.

An estimated seventy-five to one hundred thousand gators are in such captivity, with their days lazy and food assured.

The gators in the farms are indeed Florida's favorite critter, and of unquestionable economic value. Can you imagine charging tourist-rate admission to seeing cows raised? With the gator you get your money coming and going. A big alligator, as the Seminole song states, can indeed make you prosperous.

Largest of all the gator farms and attractions is Gatorland, a gator mecca on U.S. 441 outside of Orlando. It is a place where chickens are dangled in the air and fat ten-footers leap out of the water to gobble the morsel in front of hundreds of tourists.

Under a shaded walkway children pose with a baby gator, whose jaws have been carefully duct-taped. Inside,

Jimmy Tilley has high respect for gators.
His left arm bears twenty-two
stitches from wrestling a gator at Holiday Park.

cans of gator chowder, Swiss Army knives, and many types of stuffed gators fill the long green shelves. The nature of the place is summed up in the name of the great jumping event: The Gator Jumparoo. It was founded in 1949 by the late Owen Godwin, Sr., a Frank Buck type who used to love a fourteen-foot, three-inch crocodile with yellow eyes named Old Bonecrusher.

Today Gatorland comprises thirty-five acres with five thousand alligators and crocodiles, and current plans call for building an even larger park over the next two years. Buy yourself a bucket of shiners and watch the jaws of a giant alligator open and snap shut as he swirls back into the brown water. The gator feeding frenzy in *Indiana Jones and the Temple of Doom* was filmed at Gatorland.

Young gators in a temperature-controlled room.

Gator farms raise young gators in semidarkness to reduce fighting and thus produce less-scarred hides.

Drive east to St. Augustine, and only a few hundred feet from the Atlantic Ocean on Anastasia Island is the St. Augustine Alligator Farm. The farm is shaded in part by live oaks and has some of the fattest saurians great and small, including an exchange pair from the People's Republic of China. The Yangtze River is the only other part of the world that has gators. These in St. Augustine are little fellows, as is common for Chinese gators.

This is not the first gator farm in Florida. That distinction goes to the Florida Alligator Farm of Joseph ("Alligator Joe") Campbell of nearby Jacksonville, which started in 1891. It thrived on what is now one of Big Jax's numerous insurance tower grounds. The St. Augustine farm followed in 1893 after tourists in an old bathhouse out on the beach kept pestering a train engineer and showering him with quarters for the privilege of seeing gators. What resulted is one of Florida's primary tourist attractions.

Gatorland Zoo and the University of Florida have worked together for the past decade, artificially inseminating gators. One of the first gator babies born as a result of this program made the pages of People *magazine in the early 1980s.*

The gators at the St. Augustine farm—many enormous, having been in captivity since the 1930s, are fed en masse on Sundays. Bulging jowls, panzer-plated midriffs, lying sluggish in the heat—how do they ever move? Food makes some of the old reptiles frisk like puppies. A recent arrival at St. Augustine's Alligator Farm is a seventeen-foot-long saltwater crocodile that had been kept privately by an eccentric Ocala millionaire. They call the beast Gomek, and those extra few feet of tail make him seem much larger than the fat boys so well established here.

GATOR JUNGLE
IN CHRISTMAS, FLORIDA
*now claims a gator population
of 14,000.*

What family could resist a photo?

Gator attraction on U.S. 1 near Melbourne.

During the Jumparoo performance at Gatorland, gators lunge out of the water for chickens.

Because of the old farm, the city of St. Augustine might be considered the captive gator capital of Florida. Professor and "gatorman" Kent Vliet does a great deal of his live gator research here. On a National Geographic television special, Professor Vliet went into the water eyeball to eyeball with the gators for his research.

The state of Florida takes strong legal measures to regulate the farms, especially in regard to collecting eggs and hatchlings from the wild. One has to be licensed through the ears to run a gator farm. If someone ate tainted gator, why, it would be like they got food poisoning from a glass of orange juice—bad public relations for the state.

Even the Israelis are in on Florida gator farming, in a big way in a little town on Highway 50 between Disney World and Cape Canaveral. The town is Christmas, Florida, no small tourist trap itself between the giants of Goofy and rocketry.

Leaving St. Augustine, head south towards Titusville, then turn right on Highway 50 into Christmas. (You might want to avoid it during the holidays, when the town is swamped with people wanting that special postmark on their sacks of mail.)

Two gator farms are located in Christmas, but Gator Jungle, with its large gator sculpture, caters more to tourists. It was sold to an Israeli gator farming operation several years ago and is now the largest gator farm in Florida. Recently renovated, Gator Jungle now claims a gator population of fourteen thousand. While a good number of large and small gators are on display for tourists, most of that number are in growing pens as part of their gator farm operation, which is not open to the public.

Humans have turned the gator into a quasi-domesticated animal.

Meat processing at Gator Jungle. A large quantity of its frozen gator meat is shipped to Japan.

While workers move about in huge refrigerated processing trailers, general manager Kobi Kagan, who has seven years of experience in the crocodilian business, explains the expanding business: "We sold four thousand skins and fifty thousand pounds of meat last year. Some of that comes from outside our operation—we buy during the yearly hunt, and also from people around Lake Okeechobee."

Once processed, boxed, and frozen, Florida gators are finding themselves turning up on tables from Tokyo to Paris. All in all it's quite a sight to see: from the many gator tourist attractions scattered throughout the state to the multiacred farms, humans have turned the gator into a quasi-domesticated animal.

Once processed, boxed, and frozen, Florida gators are finding themselves turning up on tables from Tokyo to Paris.

*Gator Jungle alone sold 4,000 skins and
50,000 pounds of meat last year.*

Gator Lager and alligator dishes at Alligator Joe in Palm Beach.
The restaurant is filled with gator memorabilia from the early 1900s.

CHAPTER 11

ALLIGATOR JOE

Palm Beach, because of its proximity to the Gulf Stream, which comes closest to Florida shores there, had the tallest coconut

palms and was a haven for large numbers of alligators and crocodiles before it was paved over. Today the only evidence that this was so is a society (of a sort) bar and grill named Alligator Joe for a fat, famous man who ran a gator circus on the island. Joe is known to all the old-timers as the guy who ran "that tourist trap." Actually, the Florida Alligator Farm was Palm Beach's first tourist attraction, and Alligator Joe deserves a prominent place in Palm Beach history, alongside former ambassador Joe Kennedy and his sons. JFK used to hang out at Alligator Joe when it was called O'Haras.

At Joe's I find three bathrooms, one for She Gators, one for Boar Gators, and one for Sow Gators. The juke box has Elton John's *Crocodile Rock* on it but I elect to play *A Rainy Night in Georgia*. Lee Terry, managing partner of the place, gives me a Gator Lager beer brewed up in Florida's Milwaukee, Auburndale. The green longneck bottle has a picture of a cute gator wearing sunglasses with the slogan, "The Beer with a Bite."

While the engaging Mr. Terry tells tall tales about personally wrestling alligator snapping turtles, which are truly dangerous, I look at all the photographs on the wall, not all of Alligator Joe. There's the obligatory one of Jack Kennedy at his inauguration, there's the Duke and Duchess of Windsor, and there's a handsome one of George Bush lounging in a director's chair with an unidentified beautiful woman. There are a lot of unidentified beautiful Palm Beach women at the bar, none drinking Growlin' Gator Lager, but all blonde and putting your conventional Junior Leaguer to shame with their class.

The original Alligator Joe Frazier was a man with an eye for women as well as for gator. Local legend has it that he had nine wives. Lee Terry tells about the bar and grill's namesake: "Joe owned and operated a large alligator farm and wildlife circus where the Everglades Club is located

today. Seminole Indians wrestled alligators and crocodiles, and sometimes Joe would shoot a gator to the delight of the tourists."

The gator meat served up at Alligator Joe today is brought in by trapper and alligator control agent Mike Rafferty, who runs a place forty miles out, in Palm City, with the cutesy name of Alligator Bites. Actually, there are only two alligator items on the menu: Alligator Tidbits at $6.25 and the house specialty, the Fried Alligator Tail dinner, $12.95, which is served with hush puppies and other good trimmings. Tonight, Mike is the life of the bar, trying to peddle a large stuffed gator paw to the wine-sipping Palm Beach women, who are not amused. "Why, this foot comes from a thirteen-footer," says Rafferty, wearing a beeper and looking like some kind of Irish cop but really on call for nuisance gators in big Palm Beach County. "I know a dentist who uses them for ashtrays in his waiting room."

Alligator Joe is a good place. It dramatizes how far Florida has come, and perhaps the alligator paw ashtray indicates that we don't have much further to go. It's raining on the street, and with my belly full of fried gator tail I can shut my eyes in the parking lot and imagine old Alligator Joe, considered a nuisance himself by the locals, heaving his heavy-breathing frame through the mangroves after a big bull gator, to add another specimen to his collection.

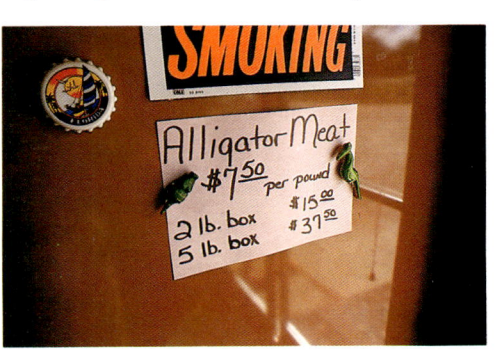

Retail gator meat prices at Gator Jungle in 1989.

CHAPTER 12

PROFESSOR GATOR

With a belly that would be politely called Falstaffian by a member of the English department, Professor Kent Vliet has a half-grin on his face and is wearing a black baseball cap with "California State SWAT Team" on it. He is a man with a mission.

"Where'd you get that cap?" I ask. "Road kill," he leers, then jumps on the back of an enraged thirteen-foot bull gator at the St. Augustine Alligator Farm, much to the horror of a pack of sun-pinked tourists standing on the elevated walkway.

Vliet, a thirty-three-year-old research biologist and professor at the University of Florida in nearby Gainesville, emerges from the green duck weed with a huge syringe and puts it between the eyes of the hyper-angry bull. The whole exercise is to determine sexual hormone levels of 175 gators living in close quarters in the lagoon of the alligator farm. An effort has been made by analyzing blood samples and even groping gator genitals to determine whether the beasts have orgasms, if so for how long, and other facts of gator reproduction.

The bull gator ridden by Vliet may not want to make love very often, but now, the needle between his eyes, he definitely wants to fight. Vliet, with his SWAT team cap in the air like a cowboy, has the gator under complete control with his lasso and his bravado. He turns the writhing beast loose in the lagoon under a rookery of wading birds. "Naw, they don't bite underwater," he hollers to a tourist on the boardwalk as the bull disappears under the duck weed. Columbus White, the cagey trapper, would disagree vehemently, and in fact Professor Vliet has taken underwater love bites and what he calls "one serious arm snag" during his work at the gator farm. He had one potentially fatal bite in the wading waters that are filled with so many big

creatures that you just naturally bump into the rather polite reptiles whether you step left or right.

Vliet is calling out data to a good-looking student assistant, botany major Danielle Davis, a South Florida woman who does this "for fun," including riding the gators. She mounts a nine-footer and appears to go into a trance sitting on its ridged "scuds" of hard leather. Dennis David, who runs the alligator hunt for the state Game and Fresh

Danielle Davis assists Vliet by keeping a tied gator quiet.

Professor Vliet and assistant getting
an uncooperative gator's blood sample.

Water Fish Commission and went on national television to proclaim that "alligators are sexy" to explain the current fixation on killing the critter, would be proud of research assistant Danielle at the St. Augustine Alligator Farm. She looks as good as Florida-born supermodel Lauren Hutton did with a gator in a *Vanity Fair* shoot for the magazine cover. "Humph," says Vliet, "Hutton's gator's got enough drugs in it to make it sleep for a week. Of course photographer Helmut Newton could not have run the risk and made it real like Danielle's."

Vliet takes a blood sample from the base of a gator's head.

Why does Vliet swim with gators, eyeball to eyeball? It's solid science and not mental illness as the tourists suggest. For one thing, it's the best way to get the alligator's point of view. For another, there is the unknown, the true lure to all scientists, about alligator courtship.

Vliet talks about the puzzle. "Courtship is obviously very dangerous for alligators. It requires them to get very close to other gators that could hurt or kill them. I went into the water to find out. The first few times I got charged. I discovered that alligators don't like to be bothered early in the morning. So I went back later in the day. First I sat down on the bank and sort of pondered what I was doing. No, I was not afraid. And gradually I moved into the water. The animals got used to me. At their level, the animals are easygoing and almost all aggression is posturing. You have to keep your eyes open, though, especially in a certain range pattern of their vision. And it requires subtlety on the part of the observer, too, yer goddamn right."

Sex in gators
is a slow, languid process
of pairs of animals coming together
and nudging, pushing and pressing along
the snout, face, head and neck
of one another.

Billboard on U.S. 301 heading toward Gainesville.

In the July heat he mops his head with his California SWAT hat. Danielle walks over with her cassette of hormone blood samples; she is streaked with brown mud from her brief ride of the gator on the bank. Vliet, after rounding up gators for three hours, also looks like he has taken a mud bath in the humid lagoon. He begins to speak tenderly of gator sex.

"A gator coming up on another in courtship approaches with its enormous back and tail submerged. It's only the eyes and snout that are visible. It's surprisingly mellow. I mean in humans sex can be like combat, but sex in gators is a slow, languid process of pairs of animals coming together and nudging, pushing, and pressing along the snout, face, head, and neck of one another. There's no

Right: *Albert the Alligator, the University of Florida mascot, gives a yell at game time.* Above: *Florida fans getting up for the game.* Bottom: *Young fan shows his allegiance.*

crocodile rock. We think of alligators as really big mean creatures, but they can be very gentle in their sexual interactions. As the affair intensifies, the gators will try to force each other underwater as a test of strength. This is an important part of a gator's decision whether to continue courtship and go ahead and mate. Like other large creatures, the alligator male must show the female that he can restrain her before she opens up for the act. Sure there are bumps and grinds, but this pushing may even stimulate the right reproductive hormones in the female."

So here we have it. Love in a crowded swamp. Thinking of old Columbus White and his wild gators over on Orange Lake, I ask the professor, "If they don't bite underwater, what would happen to you if you stepped on a copulating pair while they were underwater doing it?"

Vliet grins. "As long as it wasn't old Leaping Larry—a true nightmare of a gator out there in the lagoon who

springs without provocation. They aren't terribly aggressive animals like these tourists and people in general think they are. Of course, Leaping Larry is. Only in the hottest part of the summer and then only the largest males are willing to really come at you. At that, they really will only have the courage for one attack."

Big Kent Vliet, who as a boy was addicted to catching lizards and snakes in the grasslands around his hometown of Norman, Oklahoma, found his dream and fame in the gators of Florida. Now he is moving on to another subject, also abundant in Florida: Sharks.

MOORE HAVEN: LESS IS MORE

Sixteen miles north of the World of Sugar on U.S. 27 is a little inland port with a population of 1,272. Moore Haven, seat of Glades County

where there are many more cows and gators than people, is a special place of houses on stilts, a tree that should be Florida's most distinguished, and a quietness that will make you never want to see a highway again. Sedate Moore Haven even appeals to the young.

Take Bill Roberts, age twenty, a Georgia boy who works at Lundy's Department Store. This is an establishment that would have done for a Gabby Hayes movie set and where you can buy anything in camouflage. Bill, wearing the ubiquitous baseball hat of rural America, points to a gnarled, Japanese-looking cypress tree above the River Road. He half talks and half reads a historical marker: "The Lone Cypress has been a landmark since before the

drainage of South Florida to create prime farm land. Moore Haven grew up around the Lone Cypress, and now it's near the center of town. I've seen a photograph of it taken in 1917, and it wasn't a whole lot bigger than a palm tree."

The tree looks out over the Caloosahatchee River where it merges with Lake Okeechobee; early swamp boats would tie up to it. Look at that tree on a Sunday afternoon

when pretty girls are promenading by the river. Look a little farther out and you'll see two big old gators. This tree has witnessed all the European, Indian, and African bone-crunching efforts on the lake. God's own landmark for navigation. One historian called it "The Sentinel Cypress." Moore Haven is fortunate to still have it.

From January to March every year, bass fishers in Lake Okeechobee may enter the Chalo Nitka Fishing Contest (the strange words just mean "big bass" in Seminole). In March there is a week-long Chalo Nitka Celebration, complete with queen, fish fries, barbeques, and country music. Tours of the massive locks at Moore Haven, just under and to the right of U.S. 27's entrance bridge from the south, are possible through the lockmaster, educational for kids and adults. The easy architecture of the town will stick with you. For example, the Riverside Lodge is a remarkable Florida building, Spanish bayonets abloom in front, a two-storied rambling whitewashed wood structure like an old army building. Perhaps more than any other place, Moore Haven remains a siren, but a silent one of the mind, with a message: Come back to what Florida was.

Inset: Bass guide Tony Hussey fishing the lake out of Clewiston.
Above: Cattle ranch just north of Moore Haven.
Left: Author stops to get ice cream on the way to Moore Haven.

Sunset over Lake Okeechobee.

CHAPTER 14

MARS AND THE LEVEE AT CLEWISTON

R ichard and I are standing on the Hoover Dike levee on a hot September night when the planet Mars will come closest to

Earth in this century. Out over big brooding Lake Okeechobee there is also a full moon. A teenager in a Chevy pickup with oversized tires is firing an automatic pellet rifle into the cypress trees of the rim canal. A clump of fishers huddle in a ditch getting in one last hour of hope for something finny to take home for Sunday dinner. Gator hunters back airboats down the steep boat ramp into the canal. Lights play against the shoreline, seeking gator. Ross Hooks, the state trapper, arrives with his little official state boat and a young blond man in camouflage for yet another foray onto Lake Okeechobee. This levee on Okeechobee is where the largest number of gators were brought in during the lottery: over 550.

Quietly remote from the better-known regions of Florida, Okeechobee is a remnant of a once shallow sea called the Pamlico. A shallow, saucer-shaped lake seldom more than thirteen feet deep, it was named by the Seminoles 140 years ago when they sought refuge there from the United States Army. Their name for it was a logical one: Okeechobee means "big water." This is the queen of Florida's thirty thousand lakes and, next to Lake Michigan, is the largest expanse of fresh water wholly within the United States. It covers an area of 730 square miles, or nearly five hundred thousand acres, including the four-thousand-acre surface of three large islands: Kreamer, Torry, and Ritta. The shoreline extends 135 miles, and the mean diameter is 31 miles. Some 40 miles to the east are the palm beaches on the Atlantic; 80 miles to the west is Fort Myers and the Gulf of Mexico. You can cross Florida here by water.

The land and water of Okeechobee form one of America's most arresting scenes. Within are a vegetable kingdom, a catfish cum bass kingdom, a cattle kingdom, and a powerful agro-industrial empire that supplies Americans with 17 percent of their sugar. Okeechobee is also Florida's prime alligator water. An eighteen-footer, its tail wrapped around its head like Lady Godiva's hair, was spotted a year after the first lottery, a prime target for the next one.

At the levee, a young wildlife officer from Panama City, A. S. Hoffman, finds himself in a strange country, surrounded by old lake hunters from deeper Florida. As the mosquitoes steadily swarm in from the shallows, one old trapper tells the story of a raw Florida highway patrol officer just assigned to Clewiston after a tour of duty as a United States embassy guard in Paris. The red planet climbs toward the moon as the old man cackles.

"Somebody left the headless carcass of a twelve-foot poached gator blocking two lanes of U. S. 27 south of town, and it was raining, and this guy in the Smokey hat was scared to death, his blue lights flashing and all. He didn't even know it was a gator. Must've thought it was some kind of something escaped from a zoo headed for Miami. Hell, man, I looked at that trooper in the rain an' told him, 'Where do you think you are, man? Hell, man, this be the *Everglades* and you got this gator backing up tractor-trailers all the way to the state line.'"

Wildlife officer A. S. Hoffman checks the levee at Clewiston for any gator hunters without proper tags and permits.

A camera flash picks out gator eyes from the darkness of the water. Double reflections are caused by light from the eyes bouncing off water below.

Mars, or is it the hunt, is turning us profane. Out in the parking lot the kid with the unnerving automatic pellet rifle starts bouncing shots off trucks. We fear for our eyes. Clewiston teenagers, in automotive mating ritual, drive by in expensive Firebirds and fancy metallic pickups, then go off to pet by the local convenience store—a strange lover's lane but one where you could get a Slurpee if you got thirsty.

Another old coot tells the classic Florida tall tale of a tourist from Michigan being captured by the Seminoles up north on the lake. "They give the man one chance to live, heh, heh. They said crawl down in that ditch and make love to a gator and we'll let you go. The tourist gave it his all and accomplished the act. When he crawled out of that ditch, the Indians were all bent over laughing. 'What's so funny?' the filthy Yankee asked. 'I did what you asked, didn't I?' 'Yeah,' said the Indians, 'but you did it with the ugly one.'"

Airboats roar, the teenager fires a final burst into the tree line, and Mars begins to descend. The wildlife officer roars off to get sandwiches for his superiors. The moon, Mars, and mosquitoes on the deserted levee make me shiver in the heat. A large, saltwater-type outboard boat approaches the landing with only small running lights. Someone cranks up a pickup truck with Virginia plates and hauls in the boat.

This is it. A big late catch. There are two gators, the largest well beyond twelve feet. We recognize one of the hunters as a Coopertown man, Dale Mason, a sometime-wildman who proceeds to pick up the smaller gator and drape it around his neck for photographs. Dale looks as if he is going to blow up most of the time, a sort of Celtic Abraham Lincoln with Washington surrounded by the Confederate Army. In truth, Dale is an aircraft body repairer who lives in a little trailer on the edge of the canal at Coopertown and helps maintain the airboat fleet. He and Jesse Kennon look like brothers, Missourians afloat in the Everglades.

Dale and his partner this night of Mars pick up the big gator as a red swarm of mosquitoes actually attacks the scuds of the leathery beast. The odor of Okeechobee is everywhere. The big one wears a classic gator grin and offers no resistance, its mouth duct-taped. Brown calm eyes. Suddenly Dale's sidekick, a big German guy, black-bearded Bruce Kleinschmidt (who is about to reopen Frog City, west of Coopertown), leans down and *kisses* the monster gator passionately. Dale sees it and is pissed. He had been in the water with the beast trussing it up, and

now this sucker is kissing it for a photographer. The two men, comrades of the Okeechobee hunt, get into a fight over the thing in the pickup truck on the way back to Tamiami Trail.

I look up but can no longer see Mars for the gator blood–hungry mosquitoes. The look on the big gator's face has saddened me. By law of the lottery, he will have to be killed within twenty-four hours. Screw this whole Martian hunt, I think. To the photographer, Richard Benson, I say, "Awww, he looks like my dog Bozo with that grin."

Seriously clicking away with his Nikon and trying to clear the mosquitoes from the lens, Benson replies, "Don't think of it as Bozo. Think of it as Bozina."

We stay the whole night on the levee with its chorus of frogs almost as enthusiastic as Beethoven's "Ode to Joy." What a work of God are humans—killer angels. I actually develop chest pains over the big fellow who resembled my dog. I try to remember that this is a hunt, a hunt under Mars with harpoons and machetes and snag hooks and rope and duct tape, lots of it. Ross Hooks comes in during

the darkest part of dawn with three gators. He does a warrior kind of thing, flipping on the tape deck in his little official truck. Seminole Chief James Billie's booming voice drowns out the Okeechobee levee frog chorus:

At the age of twelve I was sure of myself
I could catch alligators by myself
But my dog didn't know what my grandpa said
He jumped in the water by the gator's head
My dog disappeared in the gator's jaw.

CHAPTER 15

FANTASY DAN AND THE DINOSAUR

Ray King, right, Jerry Metts, center, and Bubba Hanes measure gator at Mouth of the South.

Richard and I return to the shores of Okeechobee in 1989, one year after the conclusion of the first alligator harvest, or night hunt if you will. Hurricane Hugo narrowly missed the area en route to tearing up a more genteel place—Charleston —but it is nevertheless raining cats, dogs, and alligators in Clewiston. Lord, it is raining. The power goes off, and with it the lights on the Kentucky Fried Chicken sign advertising "Dark Meat Special $4.95." There is no press, of course, unless you count us and our twenty-year-old van.

We are here to do a follow-up. Although we eat our supper at the venerable Clewiston Inn, owned by U. S. Sugar Corp., it is at a smaller restaurant out toward U. S. Sugar's headquarters that we find big gators being harvested. This is in the back room of a local fish house and restaurant with the blunt name "Mouth of the South." The spartan restaurant serves excellent seafood. Along with the shrimp, catfish, and mullet, it offers something I'd never eaten: angelfish, at $1.69 a pound, same as frogs' legs. A little girl, Julia Metts, age ten, stands by the cash register passing out peppermint candy from the mouth of a stuffed gator head. There's a black bear skin on the wall, probably from North Carolina's Great Smoky Mountains.

A waitress takes us back to the slaughterhouse and ice room, where there is the usual pile of alligator heads, a

Fantasy Dan and son Heath.

73

large frozen soft-shelled turtle, and a completely intact eleven-foot gator, atop which sits Ray King, age twenty-three. The photographer and I meet a lot of felons and trustees this night of Hugo's near miss, and the harpooned gators never stop coming in. The convicts, to a man, are fine men. Ray is the bottom man at Mouth of the South tonight, and he carries a pint bottle of gin along with his eight-inch skinning and meat-slicing knife. He never complains about working the hardest and looks as if he can carry more of the tin tubs full of reddish pink chunks of meat anyway than the other men, who are drinking Michelob beer, courtesy of the boss.

That would be Jerry Metts, owner of Mouth of the South and wholesaler of catfish, bream, turtle, and alligator, according to his business card. He has good men on the job: they skin and behead a heavy twelve-footer in just an hour after Jerry's wife and another woman pick it up at Slim's Fish Camp in nearby Belle Glade. Work here will go on all night.

Workers at a marina in Clewiston point out on a map the spot where the elusive Hendrietta was last sighted. The thirteen-foot, six-inch gator that Fantasy Dan caught was believed to be the monster gator.

A gentle boy felon offers to guide us to the most famous gator hunter on the lake tonight: Fantasy Dan Collins. He is the hunter who got Hendrietta—the legendary behemoth alligator of all Florida—two days ago. The gator was named for Hendry County, in which Clewiston is the largest city and La Belle the county seat. I spot Fantasy Dan even before our guide points him out. There he stands, all 240 pounds of him, in white rubber boots and a red Mouth of the South cap. At forty-two, he is a big Georgia boy with a kind face and a twinkle to the eye. His twelve-year-old son, Heath, is helping him wash down one of two

big commercial fishing boats parked on trailers near the big trailer where he and his family live. The house trailer is only two years old, but it is marked with buckled floors, holes in the walls, and smashed windows from the rough and tumble of the commercial fishing operation. Hugo's tail winds start to act up again, and Fantasy Dan invites us inside.

"This is my oldest daughter," he says, introducing a thin girl in her teens with cerebral palsy, on the trailer floor in front of a television set watching a game show. The girl is pretty and smiles constantly. Little Heath is mesmerized by snapshots of his father with piles of dead gators. The handsome little boy had looked the same way at his father's harpoon outside. There are rolls of fishhooks everywhere, and I get some stuck on my pants, but Fantasy's wife, Betty, gently removes them with no harm done. Such is life with a big game hunter on Lake Okeechobee.

Dan's enthusiasm for the lake from which he feeds his family earned him the "Fantasy" nickname. Once Jerry Metts got three small sharks from a coastal fisher and hooked them on Dan's trout line. "Dan thought he had discovered sharks in freshwater Lake Okeechobee," Metts laughs. "He went wild and told everybody, from state Game and Fresh Water Fish to the newspapers. Let's just say he's a Georgia boy. Georgia boys tell more tall tales than Texans do, I swear." Of course, there could have been sharks in what was once the Pamlico Sea, as it is connected by canals and rivers to both the Atlantic Ocean and the Gulf of Mexico. And there are sharks in landlocked Lake Managua in Nicaragua.

I notice in Fantasy Dan's snapshots that the dead gators have bullet wounds. He must put a lot of energy into his work. In killing Hendrietta, Fantasy Dan had to shoot the gator five times with a .44 Magnum, until it stopped trying to dive and escape. "The bullets kept glancing off its skull," says Betty Collins, who had piloted the boat while her husband attacked the animal. It took nine men to lift Hendrietta onto the measuring table. The gator weighed over 800 pounds and measured thirteen feet, six inches—fifteen feet, one inch after the hide was stretched. Metts bought it for $586 and got 190 pounds of meat, about 30 pounds more than expected.

"I don't believe this was Hendrietta," Fantasy Dan says, before going back on the Hugo-agitated lake. "I've known this gator for a long time and I call him Mojo. When I harpooned him in his home in the dynamite hole, he just stood up and looked at us. This was in twenty-five to thirty feet

At Mouth of the South, two skinners work quickly, finishing a twelve-footer in an hour.

of water. No, Hendrietta's still out there in the moon vines. I definitely believe there's an eighteen-footer out there."

But Clewiston authorities dispute this. "Well, *we* think it's the one and only Hendrietta," says Game and Fresh Water Fish officer Scott Hoffman. "It's definitely the one gator they were all talking about. It's all wrinkled up around the eyes and has a humongous head. That creature's been out there on Lake Okeechobee probably eighty or ninety years. I think it was just too old and tired to fight anymore."

Fantasy Dan says there were complaints to the governor's office and that the Florida Audubon Society was riled about the killing of a venerable specimen of the state symbol. "But," he says, "gators rip my nets. When I was young I would hunt gators all night. Instead of being a baker like my daddy, I came down here to Okeechobee and I know that lake like the bottom of my hand. I'm scared of a gator like of a rabbit in my yard. Back in the old days in Georgia and Florida, we didn't use a gun. Just a hatchet. That

gator's just as scared of you as you are of him."

The squall over, we walk back outside. Fantasy Dan points at my T-shirt in the drizzle. "Gators aren't green," he says. "They're black. And for some reason they go for children and dogs. Bull gators damage the population and hunters thin them out. There's plenty of gators. Why, at night their eyes look like Christmas trees out there. Hatchlings are everywhere."

We bid the Happy Hunter good-bye, and he promises some fresh kill for us in the morning. Clewiston, except for a 7-Eleven and the slaughterhouse, is all locked up. We take an hour's sleep in the van outside the gator-skinning operation. Ray King is still working. Skinner/butcher Walt Norton has made a pile of gator feet, to be used for unusual ashtrays, etc. Large skins are rolled out and salted in the parking lot across from the East-West Elementary School. Under lazy ceiling fans, the blood is washed away for the moment.

We return to the levee where I developed chest pains a year ago over the capture of a creature we named Bozina after my dog Bozo. All is quiet except for the distant roar of airboats out on the lake. The mosquito population is tolerably low. Dawn always seems an eternity away on this vast inland sea. I wonder how many gators Fantasy Dan has caught so far and how Ray King back at Mouth of the South is doing. But then the Hendry County deputies show up on dawn patrol, one of them a shapely female wearing a uniform top, jeans, and an enormous pistol. Bass fishers begin to arrive.

Dawn cracks over Okeechobee, and with it comes an airboat with a peculiar roar, sort of like a Messerschmitt in 1944. As if in a movie, two lean men step ashore. Neither the female cop nor we journalists utter a word. One of the men has a prophet's beard. They haul two huge gators, one with a deformed face, from the airboat and heave them into a pickup truck, the tailgate of which has been bitten through by a previous "dead" gator. In the eyelids of morning, we try to talk to them. They are tight-lipped, but when we mention legendary Columbus White of Orange Lake, suspicions melt and they agree to be photographed.

"Gators come in all sizes," says one of the men, Stuart Williams of S & S Seafood in Lake Placid, "and they come in all shapes. Just like people. I thought you guys were with the Audubon Society. How's ol' Columbus? We're relatives. That was some gator he brought in from Orange Lake. Do you hear that? The noise of the airboat seems to charm them, but that's not the only noise out there. You should hear a full bull gator blowing like a freight train out there."

While his long-bearded friend, Stan Wilson of West Virginia, lashes the harpoons down in the airboat, Stuart—who reminds me of a ranger sergeant at Fort Benning—comes over with a cup of coffee in his hand. "You know God gave man dominion over the creatures of the earth," he says. The two then get into the pickup and head toward the awakening town.

We wait for Dan Collins. Dan and two friends come in late—it has been a hard night. They have only one eight-and-a-half-foot gator. "This one put up a fight," says Dan. "Couple more got away." He is breathing deeply. I look into his eyes under the Mouth of the South cap. They are so eagerly alive and human. Dan Collins himself is a fantasy, and a very good one at that.

The world is not my home, I'm only passing through . . .

Dawn breaks over the levee at Clewiston as Stuart Williams (left) and Stan Wilson bring in gators from the night's hunt.

CHAPTER 16

AN ENCOUNTER WITH THE FIRST COUSIN

The Christmas after Florida's gator hunt, I take my son and some other boys down to Flamingo to the very tip of the peninsula for five days of roughing it. I take my hunt notes, too, and am unhappy when I cannot spot a single alligator in Echo Pond because the vegetation and the skeeters have multiplied beyond endurance. Then one low tide of an afternoon, my son Josh comes dashing across a field, yelling, "Crocodile! Crocodile!"

Rushing to the gray muck of Florida Bay, I see that he and his buddy Clinton are probably right. An enormous reptile, maybe thirteen feet long and the pale green of the alligator's rare saltwater cousin, *Crocodylus acutus*, lies with his snout shoved into the roots of an ancient, rotting mangrove. To make a positive ID, I heave my middle-aged weight into the tree above the animal. The afternoon's Beck's beer does not help. My support limb snaps without even a crack, and my knees scrape the dragonlike bumps of the beast's back just as I see the narrow snout and protruding, perfectly white teeth of the American crocodile, far more dangerous than the object of the hunt. It has only one response to the airborne invasion of an awkward, showing-off father. All it does is move its slits of eyes and lock them with mine. I vamoose out of there with the prayer, "Feet don't fail me now."

A beautiful birder wearing a Vero Beach T-shirt and shooting the croc's tail with a mortar-sized lens, smiles at my antics, and I think Jeez, she looks like Bozina on Lake Okeechobee when Mars approached and I developed chest pains. She asks if I would notify the rangers of the crocodile. I nod but never make the report on one of the most potentially dangerous animals in the world. Do we have to report everything? As with the eight-foot gator on Fisheating Creek with whom I shared the rainwater, I have developed instant though wary respect for the croc. Half dreaming in my new hiker's tent that night, I marvel at my encounter with the alligator's first cousin.

The hunt or harvest, the not-really-so-great kill, had to do with the very sky and water of what remains of Florida. I can close my eyes still and see perfectly that great crocodilian predator, who visited the national park campground and then, when the tide rose, flipped its dinosaur's tail and returned to its Florida Bay territory, perhaps never to be seen by another man or little boy. But more than the exotic first cousin, I see the ordinary gator, the principal animal with which we share a land on its way to being flushed.

The sky, the water, and the creatures of the mud. I need some comfort on this star-filled night. Damn, it's dark in here away from the stars. I curse as I struggle to find my bottle of Barbancourt and canteen, as alone as an eight-foot Fisheating Creek gator drinking rainwater.

About the author

Lawrence Mahoney was born in Georgia
and grew up in the rural panhandle of Florida. A journalist
by trade, Mahoney was a Ford fellow in advanced international reporting at
Columbia University from 1970–71 and has covered events in California, Mississippi,
the Caribbean, Mexico, Germany, and Romania for *The Miami Herald*. He has
studied the Florida Everglades for twenty-five years and has one son,
Joshua Michael Mahoney, born in Miami.

About the photographer

Richard Benson met Lawrence Mahoney
while they were stationed at Fort Benning, Georgia
in 1967. Following a tour of duty in Vietnam as a photographer,
Benson returned to college and graduated from the Journalism School at the
University of Florida. He moved to New York in 1972, was on the staff at *Esquire*
magazine in the promotional art department, and then opened his own commercial
photography studio, where his work ranged from shots of celebrities to
fashion, and to jewelry. He presently lives in Miami, where he continues
his work as a photographer, and is also involved in feature
video projects as a producer and cameraman.
Gator! is his first book.